LEADING WITH THE SHEMA

A LEADER'S COMPANION TO HEAR, O ISRAEL

A COVENANT PATH™ SERIES LEADER GUIDE
BOOK 2.2

RICH VAN DOORN

To every leader who stepped forward,
not because you had all the answers,
but because you were willing to listen—and lead—in love.

Your courage to guide others toward covenant wholeness
matters more than you know.

CONTENTS

FOREWORD

If you're holding this book, you've likely said yes to something that feels bigger than you.

Maybe you're leading a small group for the first time.

Maybe you're mentoring someone one-on-one.

Maybe you still wonder if you're the right person for the job.

Let me say this clearly: **You are**.

Leading with the Shema is not written for perfect leaders. It's written for willing ones—for those who feel the weight of the Shema in their own lives and are brave enough to invite others into that same journey. The Shema isn't just a statement to memorize; it's a call to live. To love God with every part of who we are. And guiding others into that kind of love takes humility, faithfulness, and trust in the One who calls us.

This guide was designed to walk alongside you as you walk with others. Each session echoes the themes of *Hear, O Israel* and *Listening in Love*, but through the lens of leadership —offering structure, cultural insights, and practical support to help you lead with clarity and confidence.

You won't always feel adequate. That's normal. But leadership in the Kingdom of God has never been about self-assurance—it's about obedience. The best leaders are not the ones who know the most, but the ones who listen first, love well, and stay rooted in the dust of the Rabbi.

Lead with gentleness.

Lead with boldness.

And most of all, lead with the Shema ringing in your ears:

"Hear, O Israel: the Lord our God, the Lord is one."

—Rich Van Doorn

WALKING THE WAY OF THE RABBI — ONE BOOK, ONE STEP AT A TIME

Your Journey Has Begun...

This Leader Guide — *Guiding in the Dust* — is the next step in a 17-book discipleship journey.

Each book in *The Covenant Path*™ series is paired with:

- A **Core Book** – Theological and historical foundations
- A **Devotional** – Six-day spiritual practice + Sabbath reflection
- A **Leader Guide** – Cultural insights, Hebraic terms, and small group support

THE COVENANT PATH™ SERIES (CONFIRMED TITLES & SUBTITLES)

1. **Dustprints of the Rabbi:** *Discipleship in the Texture of Torah and Grace*

HOW TO KEEP WALKING

Each step includes:

- A teaching book
- A companion devotional
- A leader guide like this one

Start with the next title — or gather a new group to walk through this one again.

Discipleship is not a class. It's a path. The Rabbi is still walking. So must we.

INTRODUCTION: LEADING WITH THE SHEMA

You are not just holding a guide.

You are stepping into the ancient role of a *talmid-maker*—one who walks alongside others in the dust of discipleship.

Leading with the Shema is a 12-session leadership companion designed to help you guide others through *Hear, O Israel: Living the Shema in a World of Competing Voices* and its devotional counterpart, *Listening in Love*. It's more than a discussion outline. It's a covenant tool for shaping identity, loyalty, and obedience in a world of spiritual drift.

Each week, you'll walk with your group through the ancient words of the Shema and the living story of the Messiah who embodied it. You'll lead not with mastery, but with movement—not by explaining everything, but by modeling faithful presence.

This guide is grounded in the rhythms of Jewish-Christian discipleship. You'll encounter Torah principles, Hebraic terms, Mishnah and Midrash insights, and rich cultural context—not as academic detours, but as spiritual anchors. Every session is designed to help your group not just talk about the Shema, but *live* it.

WHAT TO EXPECT EACH WEEK

Each session follows the same rhythm and structure that shaped *Guiding in the Dust*, the leader guide for *Dustprints of the Rabbi*. Your weekly framework includes:

1. **Focus Verse** — the Scripture anchor from the Shema or the teachings of Jesus
2. **Theme** — a covenant truth to guide the discussion
3. **Leader Objective** — a summary of what participants should walk away with
4. **Opening Prayer & Shema** — space to pray and recite the Shema aloud
5. **Grounding in the Dust** — Hebraic insight and cultural context, often with Mishnah or Midrash
6. **Recap & Reflection** — highlights from *Hear, O Israel* and *Listening in Love*
7. **Group Discussion Questions** — 4–6 prompts to foster depth and dialogue
8. **Dustprint Discipleship Challenge** — a tangible call to action
9. **Closing Prayer & Group Blessing** — to seal each session in unity and surrender

TO THE LEADER WALKING THE PATH

Your role is sacred. Not because you have all the answers—but because you've said "yes" to guiding others on the path of covenant love. You are walking with your group not as a tour guide, but as a fellow traveler.

As you prepare each week:

- Pray for your people by name
- Soak in the chapter and devotional content
- Ask the Spirit to guide your tone and timing
- Let the Shema shape you first—then lead from overflow

This journey will not be linear. It will be layered. Some weeks will feel light; others will stir deep wrestling. But every session is a chance to listen again. To walk again. To return again.

Because the Shema is not only spoken—it is lived.

And you are leading the way.

LEADER COVENANT &
COMMITMENT

WALKING IN THE DUST TOGETHER

"Whoever wants to be great among you must be your servant."

— MATTHEW 20:26

As a leader on The Covenant Path™, I commit to:

1. Walk Behind the Rabbi First

I will lead not from arrival, but from pursuit. I will walk behind Jesus — not just talk about Him. My leadership will flow from discipleship.

2. Create Space for Formation

I will foster environments where others can wrestle, wonder, listen, and grow. I will lead with grace, humility, and spiritual curiosity.

3. Honor the Hebraic Roots of Our Faith

I will approach this journey with reverence for the Jewish worldview of Jesus and the first-century context of His teaching. I will define terms, invite questions, and point others to the richness of Scripture in its original setting.

4. Uphold Unity and Confidentiality

I will protect the sacred space of group conversations. What is shared in the group stays in the group, unless there is a need for loving accountability or safety.

5. Practice What I Facilitate

I will not call others to a path I am unwilling to walk myself. I will engage the devotional, reflect on the book, and live out the truth I ask others to explore.

6. Pray Before I Plan

I will lead prayerfully, not just practically. I will ask the Spirit of the Rabbi to guide each session and each heart — including mine.

LEADER COVENANT AFFIRMATION

Name: ____

Date: ____

"Rabbi Jesus, I offer You my steps, my words, my silence, and my leadership. May I guide others only as I follow You. Let my feet stay in the dust, and let those who follow me find You there. Amen."

HOW TO USE THIS GUIDE

This guide is a map—but not a map to control the journey. It's a guide to help you walk with others through the sacred terrain of covenant love.

Each session in *Leading with the Shema* is aligned with *Hear, O Israel: Living the Shema in a World of Competing Voices* and its devotional companion, *Listening in Love*. This is not just a curriculum—it's a rhythm of remembrance, reflection, and response. It's how we help others move from hearing the Shema to living it with wholeness.

Whether you're gathering in a living room, a sanctuary, or a discipleship circle, this guide is meant to help you create space for transformation.

WHAT YOU'LL FIND IN EVERY SESSION

Each of the 12 sessions follows a consistent, leader-friendly rhythm:

1. **Focus Verse** — a Shema-rooted Scripture to anchor the session
2. **Theme** — a single-line truth that captures the week's message
3. **Leader Objective** — what participants will reflect on, wrestle with, or carry forward
4. **Opening Prayer & Shema** — space to invite God's voice and re-center in the Shema
5. **Grounding in the Dust** — historical, linguistic, or cultural insights from Jewish tradition
6. **Recap & Reflection** — key connections from *Hear, O Israel* and *Listening in Love*
7. **Group Discussion Questions** — 4–6 questions to foster vulnerability and depth
8. **Dustprint Discipleship Challenge** — one tangible action for covenant application
9. **Closing Prayer & Group Blessing** — to send participants out with unity and intention

A FEW TIPS FOR LEADING WELL

- **Start with the Spirit.** Don't just prep questions—pray for your group. Ask the Spirit to speak louder than your outline.
- **Honor the Hebraic rhythm.** This isn't Western lecture-based learning. It's dialogue, walking, and wrestling. Let the room breathe. Let silence speak.
- **Model what you want multiplied.** Vulnerability begets vulnerability. If you're honest, others will be too.
- **Let the format serve you.** Don't rush through every section. Let the Spirit highlight what your group needs most that week.

- **Keep returning to the Shema.** Speak it aloud. Let it frame your gatherings. Let it become a rhythm that lingers long after the session ends.

PAIRING THIS GUIDE WITH THE DEVOTIONAL

If your group is also using *Listening in Love*, create time for devotional reflection each week. Consider opening each session with the question:

"What moment from the devotional shaped you this week?"

This creates a deeper connection between reading, reflection, and communal living.

YOUR ROLE AS COVENANT GUIDE

You are not the expert. You are the guide in the dust. The one who says, "Let's walk this together." You won't have all the answers—but you'll carry the right questions. And that's enough.

So lead with patience. With presence. And with courage.

"Hear, O Israel..."

The words were never just for the ancient camp.
They are for your group.
For your living room.
For this generation.

You're not just leading a study.
You're helping others live the Shema.

SESSION 1: HEAR AND OBEY

THE BIBLICAL MEANING OF TRUE HEARING

Focus Verse

"Hear, O Israel: The Lord our God, the Lord is one."

— DEUTERONOMY 6:4

Theme: True hearing in Hebraic thought always leads to responsive obedience. The Shema is not heard until it is lived.

Leader Objective: By the end of this session, group members will be able to define the Hebraic meaning of *shema*, reflect on Jesus' use of the Shema in His teachings, and identify one area where hearing God's Word must move into obedient action.

1. OPENING PRAYER & SHEMA

Prayer Prompt:

Father, we don't want to be hearers only. We want to be followers—people who listen with our lives. Help us not to treat Your voice as background noise, but as the rhythm of covenant love.

Amen.

Optional Shema (Deuteronomy 6:4–5):

"Hear, O Israel: The LORD our God, the LORD is one.

Love the LORD your God with all your heart and with all your soul and with all your strength."

---

2. GROUNDING IN THE DUST (CULTURAL INSIGHT)

The Hebrew word *shema* (שמע) means far more than "listen." It also implies obedience, attention, and alignment. In Jewish tradition, to hear without obeying was to not truly hear at all.

In the first-century world of Jesus, this connection was assumed. A rabbi's words were meant to be enacted. The concept of hearing and not doing would have seemed absurd.

Mishnah Insight:

"It is not the learning that is the main thing, but the doing."

— AVOT 1:17

In the Shema, God is not inviting polite contemplation. He is issuing a covenant call. To hear is to respond. And to recite the Shema daily was to rehearse obedience every morning and night.

Hebraic Terms Introduced This Week:

- **Shema** – To hear, pay attention, and obey in one unified act.
- **Avodah** – Service or worship; the action of love in the Hebrew mind.
- **Levav** – Heart; not just emotion, but the center of thought, desire, and will.

3. RECAP & REFLECTION (BOOK + DEVOTIONAL HIGHLIGHTS)

Book Recap – Hear, O Israel (Chapter 1):
Hearing was the first step in Israel's covenant. Before laws were given, before the land was possessed, the people were invited to listen—and to respond. This chapter explores how *shema* shapes every act of discipleship, not as obligation but as relational response. Jesus affirms this by quoting the Shema as the greatest commandment.

Devotional Tie-In – Listening in Love (Week 1):
This week's entries unpacked what it means to "listen in love." From ancient Israel to Jesus' teaching in Matthew 7, the reflections traced the transformation that begins when hearing becomes action. Day 3 introduced a Mishnah insight on learning and doing, while Day 4 told the story of Maya—a woman who obeyed God's whisper even when it disrupted

her plans.

4. GROUP DISCUSSION QUESTIONS

You don't need to use all of these. Choose 4–6 that best fit your group's tone and time.

1. *What stood out to you from the book or devotional this week?*
2. *How would you define "hearing" in your own words, based on what you've read?*
3. *Why do you think shema links hearing with obedience in Hebrew thought?*
4. *What's an area in your life where you've been hearing but not obeying?*
5. *How does Jesus' use of the Shema challenge your understanding of discipleship?*
6. *What do you think it means to obey before you fully understand?*

Invite your group to take one clear, visible step of obedience this week—something they've heard God speak but haven't yet done.

Challenge Prompt (from Devotional):
"Take one tangible action that moves from hearing to doing.Let obedience be your first act of love."

Examples:

- Initiate a difficult conversation.
- Confess something you've been hiding.
- Begin a rhythm of prayer you've delayed.

Ask group members to reflect next week on how it went.

6. CLOSING PRAYER & GROUP BLESSING

Prayer Prompt:

God, You are not silent.
You have spoken through prophets, Scripture, and
through Jesus our Messiah.
Now speak again—into our hearts, our choices, and
our steps.
May we not only hear, but obey.
Amen.

OPTIONAL GROUP BLESSING (SPOKEN TOGETHER):

"We hear the voice of the Lord—and we respond
with love.
We walk in obedience—and we do not walk alone."

SESSION 2: LOVING WITH ALL THE HEART

COVENANT LOYALTY THROUGH EMOTIONAL DEVOTION

FOCUS VERSE

"Love the Lord your God with all your heart..."

— DEUTERONOMY 6:5A

Theme: Covenant love begins with a loyal heart—devotion that includes not just feeling, but the full alignment of desire, thought, and will.

Leader Objective: By the end of this session, group members will be able to define the Hebraic meaning of "heart," examine their personal affections and loyalties, and identify one shift that would move them toward greater covenant devotion.

1. OPENING PRAYER & SHEMA

Prayer Prompt:

Lord, You are not asking for half our hearts. You're calling for all of us—every desire, thought, and longing. Help us to examine what we love most, and return our hearts fully to You.

Amen.

Optional Shema (Deuteronomy 6:4–5):

"Hear, O Israel: The LORD our God, the LORD is one.

Love the LORD your God with all your heart and with all your soul and with all your strength."

---

2. GROUNDING IN THE DUST (CULTURAL INSIGHT)

In biblical Hebrew, the word for heart is *levav* (לְבָב), which includes not only emotion but the seat of intellect, decision-making, and will. To love God "with all your heart" means to love Him with your entire inner being.

In Jewish thought, loyalty is a key expression of love. The heart was not seen as a place of fleeting emotion, but as the control center of a person's life.

Mishnah Insight:

"Make His will your will, so that He may make your will His."

— AVOT 2:4

This is what it means to love God with the heart—not just when it's easy, but when it requires surrender of our inner preferences and competing affections.

Hebraic Terms Introduced This Week:

- **Levav** – Heart; the core of a person's will, desires, and decisions
- **Ahavah** – Love; not only emotional, but covenantal and loyal
- **Yetzer** – Inclination; inner desire, either toward God (*yetzer hatov*) or away (*yetzer hara*)

3. RECAP & REFLECTION (BOOK + DEVOTIONAL HIGHLIGHTS)

Book Recap – Hear, O Israel (Chapter 2):
Loving God with all the heart calls us beyond emotion into covenant loyalty. This chapter explores the biblical understanding of heart as the command center of our lives. It reminds us that Shema-formed love is an active surrender of will, not a sentimental moment.

Devotional Tie-In – Listening in Love (Week 2):
This week's reflections focused on returning to our "first love" and reordering our affections around God. Day 3 introduced a Mishnah insight about aligning our will with God's, and Day 4 told the story of Elijah—who, in the face of devastating news, chose to love God even when the outcome was unclear.

4. GROUP DISCUSSION QUESTIONS

Choose 4–6 questions that best fit your group's tone and time:

1. *What stood out to you from the book or devotional this week?*
2. *How do you understand the idea of the heart in Hebraic thought?*
3. *What competes with your love for God at the level of desire?*
4. *Can you recall a time when your emotions aligned—or collided—with obedience?*
5. *What does it mean to love God when you don't "feel" it?*
6. *What would it look like to surrender your will more fully to Him this week?*

5. DUSTPRINT DISCIPLESHIP CHALLENGE

Challenge your group to realign one internal affection this week toward covenant love.

Challenge Prompt (from Devotional):
"Choose one act of loyalty this week that reflects deep heart love—not fleeting emotion."

Examples:

- Forgive someone who doesn't deserve it
- Confess an area of misaligned desire
- Set a boundary that protects your spiritual health

Ask them to reflect next week on how this shift felt—and what it revealed.

6. CLOSING PRAYER & GROUP BLESSING

Prayer Prompt:

Father, search our hearts.
We want to love You with all of who we are—not
*   just in emotion, but in loyalty.*
Help us align our desires with Your will.
And lead us to love You first, most, and always.
Amen.

OPTIONAL GROUP BLESSING (SPOKEN TOGETHER):

"We love the Lord our God with all our heart.
He is One—and we are His."

SESSION 3: LOVING WITH ALL THE SOUL

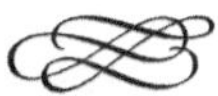

TRUSTING GOD WITH LIFE ITSELF

Focus Verse

"Love the Lord your God with all your soul..."

— DEUTERONOMY 6:5B

Theme: To love God with all your soul is to entrust Him with your entire being—your breath, your identity, and your existence.

Leader Objective: By the end of this session, group members will be able to define the Hebraic meaning of *soul* (*nephesh*), reflect on what it means to entrust their life to God, and identify one step of surrender that affirms their covenant love.

1. OPENING PRAYER & SHEMA

Prayer Prompt:

Lord, You gave us breath. You know every part of who we are— what we carry, what we hide, what we fear. Teach us to love You with our whole soul today, and trust You with everything we are.

Amen.

Optional Shema (Deuteronomy 6:4–5):

"Hear, O Israel: The LORD our God, the LORD is one.

Love the LORD your God with all your heart and with all your soul and with all your strength."

---

2. GROUNDING IN THE DUST (CULTURAL INSIGHT)

In Hebrew, the word for soul is *nephesh* (נֶפֶשׁ), which does not mean "the invisible spirit" as in Greek philosophy, but the entire living being. To love God with all your *nephesh* is to love Him with your life—your breath, your body, your identity, your future.

In Jewish thought, this is often linked to *mesirut nefesh*— "giving of the soul"—which came to mean surrendering one's whole life, even to the point of martyrdom if necessary.

Talmud Insight:

"A man should love God with all his soul—even if He takes your soul."

— BERAKHOT 61B

In Jesus' day, this wasn't just a theoretical ideal. Many first-century Jews lived under foreign rule, where loyalty to God meant risking your life. To love God with all your soul was to say, "My life belongs to You—even when I don't know what comes next."

Hebraic Terms Introduced This Week:

- **Nephesh** – Soul; the whole living being
- **Mesirut Nefesh** – Self-sacrifice; surrendering one's soul for God
- **Ruach** – Spirit or breath; what gives life to the body

3. RECAP & REFLECTION (BOOK + DEVOTIONAL HIGHLIGHTS)

Book Recap – Hear, O Israel (Chapter 3):
This chapter unpacks how loving God with your soul involves surrendering your identity, desires, and even your fears. It's not about detaching from life, but offering your whole self back to the One who formed you.

Devotional Tie-In – Listening in Love (Week 3):
Daily reflections explored the tension between trust and surrender. Day 3 featured the Talmudic insight on loving God even unto death, while Day 4 told Lina's story—a woman who whispered the Shema beside her son's hospital bed, not as a formula, but as a declaration of trust when everything else was unclear.

4. GROUP DISCUSSION QUESTIONS

Choose 4–6 questions that best fit your group's flow:

1. *What stood out to you this week from the book or devotional?*
2. *How is the Hebraic view of "soul" different from our typical understanding?*
3. *What would it look like for you to love God with your whole life—not just your beliefs?*
4. *Where have you been holding back part of your soul from God?*
5. *How do trust and surrender work together in loving God with all your soul?*
6. *What does mesirut nefesh look like for you in this season?*

5. DUSTPRINT DISCIPLESHIP CHALLENGE

Invite your group to surrender something real and personal this week—an area of identity, control, or fear.

Challenge Prompt (from Devotional):
"Offer God your whole life—not just in theory, but in tangible trust."

Examples:

- Release a fear in prayer
- Speak truth where silence has reigned
- Give generously from what feels scarce
- Recommit to something God asked you to carry

Encourage group members to reflect on what happened —and how it felt.

6. CLOSING PRAYER & GROUP BLESSING

Prayer Prompt:

God, we give You our lives—not just our words. Our breath is Yours. Our future is Yours. Our broken places and our dreams are Yours. Teach us to love You with everything we are.

Amen.

OPTIONAL GROUP BLESSING (SPOKEN TOGETHER):

*"We love the Lord our God with all our soul.
He gave us breath—and we give Him our trust."*

SESSION 4: LOVING WITH ALL THE STRENGTH

TOTAL-LIFE DISCIPLESHIP

Focus Verse

"Love the Lord your God with all your... strength."

— DEUTERONOMY 6:5C

Theme: To love God with all your strength is to offer Him your capacity, your "muchness," and every resource entrusted to you.

Leader Objective: By the end of this session, group members will be able to explain the Hebrew meaning of "strength" (*me'od*), assess how they use their time, energy, and resources, and identify one way to love God with greater intentionality this week.

1. OPENING PRAYER & SHEMA

Prayer Prompt:
Lord, You've given us more than enough. You've filled our lives with time, strength, and resources—not just for our benefit, but for Your glory. Teach us to love You with our "muchness."
Amen.

Optional Shema (Deuteronomy 6:4–5):
"Hear, O Israel: The LORD our God, the LORD is one.
Love the LORD your God with all your heart and with all your soul and with all your strength."

---

2. GROUNDING IN THE DUST (CULTURAL INSIGHT)

The Hebrew word translated "strength" in the Shema is *me'od* (מְאֹד), which more literally means "muchness" or "abundance." It refers not just to physical strength, but to your capacity—your energy, possessions, influence, and effort.

In ancient Israel, this wasn't about performance but **offering the fullness of what God entrusted to you.**

Midrash Insight:
"You shall love Him... with your wealth, with your possessions, with your every measure."

— SIFRE DEVARIM 32:3

To love God with *me'od* is to love Him with everything you carry: not just your body, but your budget, your bandwidth, your platform—your ability to act.

Jesus echoed this when He said, "Where your treasure is, there your heart will be also" (Matthew 6:21).

Hebraic Terms Introduced This Week:

- **Me'od** – Strength; fullness, abundance, "muchness"
- **Koach** – Power or ability
- **Avodah** – Work or worship; the way your effort becomes an offering

3. RECAP & REFLECTION (BOOK + DEVOTIONAL HIGHLIGHTS)

Book Recap – Hear, O Israel (Chapter 4):
This chapter explores how the Shema calls us to an embodied faith—one that doesn't just believe but acts. Loving God with our strength means living a faith that shows up in our time, our work, and our willingness to give.

Devotional Tie-In – Listening in Love (Week 4):
The week's devotional reflections emphasized how "strength" includes more than effort—it's about investment. Day 3 included a Midrash teaching about loving God with all your measures, and Day 4 told the story of Marcus—a man who learned that even empty hands can be surrendered in love.

4. GROUP DISCUSSION QUESTIONS

Choose 4–6 questions that best fit your group:

1. *What stood out to you in the book or devotional this week?*
2. *How does the meaning of me'od shift your view of "strength"?*
3. *What resources—time, money, energy, ability—are you holding back from God?*
4. *When do you feel most stretched in your discipleship?*
5. *How do you discern whether you're offering your best or your leftovers?*
6. *What would a lifestyle of total-life worship look like for you this week?*

5. DUSTPRINT DISCIPLESHIP CHALLENGE

Invite your group to choose one part of their "muchness" to offer God this week.

Challenge Prompt (from Devotional):
"Give God your strength by offering Him something costly—and something beautiful."

Examples:

- Serve someone with no spotlight
- Give financially to someone in need
- Use your gifts for Kingdom work outside your comfort zone
- Rest in a way that honors God with margin and trust

Encourage reflection the following week on how it stretched or renewed them.

6. CLOSING PRAYER & GROUP BLESSING

Prayer Prompt:*Lord, You've given us much—more than we often admit. Teach us not just to love You in word, but in offering. Help us surrender our time, our effort, our energy, and our resources. May our strength become worship.*
Amen.

OPTIONAL GROUP BLESSING (SPOKEN TOGETHER):

"We love the Lord our God with all our strength.

With our effort, our offering, and our every measure—we worship Him."

SESSION 5: WRITE IT ON YOUR HEART

INTERNALIZING THE TORAH FOR EVERYDAY LIFE

Focus Verse

"These commandments that I give you today are to be on your hearts."

— DEUTERONOMY 6:6

Theme: God's Word is not just meant to be heard—it's meant to be engraved on the heart, forming a life that walks in rhythm with His voice.

Leader Objective: By the end of this session, group members will be able to describe the significance of internalizing the Word in Hebraic thought, examine what voices shape their inner world, and commit to one practice that helps write Scripture on their heart.

1. OPENING PRAYER & SHEMA

Prayer Prompt:
God, we don't just want to read Your Word—we want to be shaped by it. Engrave Your truth on our hearts until it changes how we think, speak, and live.
Amen.

Optional Shema (Deuteronomy 6:4–5):
"Hear, O Israel: The LORD our God, the LORD is one.
Love the LORD your God with all your heart and with all your soul and with all your strength."

---

2. GROUNDING IN THE DUST (CULTURAL INSIGHT)

In Hebraic thought, the heart (*levav*) is not only the seat of emotion, but of memory, thought, and decision-making. To "write the commandments on your heart" means to internalize them until they shape your instincts, values, and reflexes.

In ancient Israel, oral recitation and repetition were key tools for heart-engraving. Scripture was memorized in community, spoken aloud, sung, and repeated across generations.

Mishnah Insight:

"He who repeats a chapter one hundred times is not like him who repeats it one hundred and one."

— CHAGIGAH 9B

The power of repetition wasn't academic—it was formative. You return to what matters so it becomes part of who you are.

Hebraic Terms Introduced This Week:

- **Levav** – Heart; mind, will, emotion, and inner life
- **Zakar** – To remember; not just mental recall, but covenant action
- **Shamar** – To keep, guard, or preserve (used of God's commandments)

3. RECAP & REFLECTION (BOOK + DEVOTIONAL HIGHLIGHTS)

Book Recap – Hear, O Israel (Chapter 5):
This chapter reminds us that God doesn't want external compliance—He desires internal transformation. The Shema was always meant to be written on the heart. Not just memorized, but embodied. Not just studied, but stored.

Devotional Tie-In – Listening in Love (Week 5):
The devotional reflections emphasized the role of repetition, saturation, and memory. Day 3 highlighted the Mishnah teaching on repetition, and Day 4 told the story of Ella—a

woman who carried Psalm 27:1 in her pocket until it rewrote her inner world.

4. GROUP DISCUSSION QUESTIONS

Choose 4–6 questions that resonate most with your group:

1. *What stood out to you this week in the book or devotional?*
2. *How does the Hebraic view of "heart" reshape how you understand internal transformation?*
3. *What voices or messages are currently shaping your inner world?*
4. *How do you currently engage with Scripture—reading, memorizing, meditating?*
5. *What verse or truth do you want God to engrave more deeply on your heart?*
6. *What would a "saturated" life in the Word look like in your context?*

5. DUSTPRINT DISCIPLESHIP CHALLENGE

Challenge your group to internalize one passage of Scripture this week—not for information, but transformation.

Challenge Prompt (from Devotional):
"Choose one verse to carry with you—physically and spiritually—this week. Let it rewrite something in you."

Examples:

- Write it on a sticky note or notecard
- Set it as your phone lock screen
- Recite it aloud each morning and night

- Reflect on it during daily tasks

Encourage group members to share what changed by next session.

6. CLOSING PRAYER & GROUP BLESSING

Prayer Prompt:
Lord, write Your Word on our hearts—not in ink, but in Spirit. Let it become our first thought in trouble, our guide in confusion, and our anchor in temptation. May Your truth live inside us.
Amen.

Optional Group Blessing (spoken together):

"We write His Word on our hearts—and walk with covenant wholeness.
We are His, and He is One."

SESSION 6: TEACH IT TO YOUR CHILDREN

MULTI-GENERATIONAL DISCIPLESHIP

Focus Verse

"Impress them on your children. Talk about them when you sit at home..."

— DEUTERONOMY 6:7A

Theme: The Shema was never meant to stay personal—it was designed to be passed down through daily, relational discipleship.

Leader Objective: By the end of this session, group members will be able to describe the Shema's call to generational faithfulness, identify who they are influencing spiritually (whether or not they are parents), and commit to one intentional act of faith transmission this week.

1. OPENING PRAYER & SHEMA

Prayer Prompt:
Father, You are the God of generations. Teach us how to pass on what You've given us—not just through words, but through example. Help us disciple those around us with love, presence, and purpose.
Amen.

Optional Shema (Deuteronomy 6:4–5):
"Hear, O Israel: The LORD our God, the LORD is one.
Love the LORD your God with all your heart and with all your soul and with all your strength."

---

2. GROUNDING IN THE DUST (CULTURAL INSIGHT)

In the ancient Hebrew world, teaching children wasn't left to formal education—it was woven into the rhythms of home life. The word used in Deuteronomy 6:7 for "impress" (Hebrew: *shanan*) means to sharpen, engrave, or etch deeply. Teaching God's Word was meant to be repetitive, relational, and rhythmic.

Talmud Insight:
"He who teaches his child, it is as if he had taught his child's child, and so on to the end of generations."

— KIDDUSHIN 30A

Teaching the next generation wasn't just about content. It was about legacy. In fact, the Shema became the first Scripture Jewish children memorized. Faith was passed down not only by what was said, but by how it was lived.

Hebraic Terms Introduced This Week:

- **Shanan** – To impress, engrave, or sharpen
- **Dor v'dor** – "From generation to generation"
- **Bayit** – House or household; center of faith transmission in Jewish life

3. RECAP & REFLECTION (BOOK + DEVOTIONAL HIGHLIGHTS)

Book Recap – Hear, O Israel (Chapter 6):
This chapter explores how the Shema prioritizes intergenerational faithfulness. Teaching children was never a passive act—it was active, embedded into daily life. It challenges us to see spiritual formation as a household responsibility, not just a communal one.

Devotional Tie-In – Listening in Love (Week 6):
The devotional reflections focused on how our homes and habits teach as much as our words. Day 3 featured a Talmudic teaching on generational impact, and Day 4 shared the story of Jamie—a woman who never forgot her grandmother's prayer posture and later adopted it as her own.

4. GROUP DISCUSSION QUESTIONS

Choose 4–6 questions that fit your group:

1. *What stood out to you from the reading or devotional this week?*
2. *How does "teaching" in the Shema differ from modern ideas of education?*
3. *Who are the people God has placed in your life for spiritual influence?*
4. *What kind of atmosphere do you create in your home or relationships?*
5. *What small habits have you witnessed that shaped your faith long-term?*
6. *What legacy do you hope your life is passing on—intentionally or not?*

5. DUSTPRINT DISCIPLESHIP CHALLENGE

Encourage your group to take one intentional step of faith transmission this week—especially in relational, everyday ways.

Challenge Prompt (from Devotional):
"Speak one blessing, share one story, or model one habit that reflects the Shema in your home or community."

Examples:

- Pray a blessing over a child or friend
- Share a personal faith story with someone younger
- Begin a spiritual rhythm in your household (Scripture, gratitude, prayer)

Encourage follow-up reflection in the next session.

6. CLOSING PRAYER & GROUP BLESSING

Prayer Prompt:
Lord, make us faithful teachers—whether we're parents, siblings, mentors, or friends. Help us engrave Your truth in those around us. Let our homes become sanctuaries where the Shema is lived and loved.
Amen.

Optional Group Blessing (spoken together):

"We impress His words on the next generation.
From our homes to our habits, from our lips to our legacy —we speak the Shema."

SESSION 7: BIND IT ON YOUR HANDS

LIVING FAITH THROUGH VISIBLE ACTION

Focus Verse

"Tie them as symbols on your hands..."

— DEUTERONOMY 6:8A

Theme: Discipleship isn't just about belief—it's about visible, embodied action that reflects covenant love.

Leader Objective: By the end of this session, group members will be able to explain the significance of binding the Word to the hands in Hebraic thought, reflect on how their actions display their faith, and identify one area where they can visibly live out obedience this week.

1. OPENING PRAYER & SHEMA

Prayer Prompt:
Lord, let our hands reflect our hearts. We want our actions to echo our allegiance—faith not just spoken, but seen. Help us live what we believe.
Amen.

Optional Shema (Deuteronomy 6:4–5):
"Hear, O Israel: The LORD our God, the LORD is one.
Love the LORD your God with all your heart and with all your soul and with all your strength."

---

2. GROUNDING IN THE DUST (CULTURAL INSIGHT)

In Jewish tradition, Deuteronomy 6:8 is the basis for the practice of wearing *tefillin*—small leather boxes containing Scripture passages, bound to the hand and forehead during prayer. While symbolic, the intent was deeply formative: the Word was meant to shape both action (hand) and thought (head).

Midrash Insight:
"Just as one wears tefillin and is reminded of the commandments, so too let the hand be a reminder through deeds."

— TANCHUMA, TZAV 14

In other words, the outward symbol was never the point —the **visible obedience** was. In Hebraic thought, the hand represents action, agency, and will. What you do matters— and how you do it speaks volumes.

Hebraic Terms Introduced This Week:

- **Tefillin** – Phylacteries; small boxes tied to arm/forehead containing Torah texts
- **Ma'aseh** – Deed or action; the lived outcome of belief
- **Avodah** – Work as worship; embodied obedience

3. RECAP & REFLECTION (BOOK + DEVOTIONAL HIGHLIGHTS)

Book Recap – Hear, O Israel (Chapter 7):
This chapter examines how the Shema calls us to live our faith in a way that can be seen. Binding the Word on your hands isn't about ritual—it's about visibility. Faith becomes real when it's embodied, consistent, and visible to others.

Devotional Tie-In – Listening in Love (Week 7):
The week's reflections focused on how our hands tell the truth about our hearts. Day 3 explored Midrashic teaching on tefillin and deeds, while Day 4 told the story of Teresa—a woman whose simple acts of service quietly preached the Gospel in her neighborhood.

4. GROUP DISCUSSION QUESTIONS

Select 4–6 questions that best fit your group's tone and time:

1. *What impacted you most from the chapter or devotional this week?*
2. *What does "binding God's Word on your hands" mean in everyday terms?*
3. *How do you discern when your actions reflect obedience —or convenience?*
4. *What does visible obedience look like in your workplace, home, or neighborhood?*
5. *When has someone's ma'aseh (deed) impacted your faith?*
6. *Where is God calling you to make your obedience more visible?*

5. DUSTPRINT DISCIPLESHIP CHALLENGE

Encourage your group to take one visible step of obedience this week—no spotlight, just faith in action.

Challenge Prompt (from Devotional):
"Let your hands preach. Choose an act of obedience that others can see—not for applause, but for love."

Examples:

- Serve someone anonymously
- Repair something broken (physically or relationally)
- Complete a task with integrity when shortcuts tempt
- Offer help or hospitality in a new way

Next week, invite reflections on how obedience changed the atmosphere.

6. CLOSING PRAYER & GROUP BLESSING

Prayer Prompt:
Lord, bind Your Word to our hands. May our deeds declare Your goodness, our actions reflect Your truth, and our strength be surrendered in service. Let us love You with what we do.
Amen.

Optional Group Blessing (spoken together):

"We bind His words to our hands.
Our faith is seen, our actions aligned, and our hands reflect His heart."

SESSION 8: SPEAK OF IT IN YOUR HOME

BUILDING TORAH-CENTERED HOUSEHOLDS

Focus Verse

"Talk about them when you sit at home and when you walk along the road..."

— DEUTERONOMY 6:7B

Theme: The home is the first altar of discipleship—where faith is made real through daily conversation, ordinary rhythms, and consistent presence.

Leader Objective: By the end of this session, group members will be able to describe the Shema's vision for home-centered discipleship, reflect on the spiritual atmosphere of their home, and identify one way to make Scripture more present in their daily life.

1. OPENING PRAYER & SHEMA

Prayer Prompt:
Lord, we open not just our mouths, but our homes. Make our living spaces holy places—where Your truth is spoken, remembered, and lived. Let Your Word dwell with us.
Amen.

Optional Shema (Deuteronomy 6:4–5):
"Hear, O Israel: The LORD our God, the LORD is one.
Love the LORD your God with all your heart and with all your soul and with all your strength."

---

2. GROUNDING IN THE DUST (CULTURAL INSIGHT)

In the time of Moses and again in the days of Jesus, the home (*bayit*) was the primary place of spiritual formation. Discipleship was not delegated to synagogues alone—it happened at the table, on the road, in rising and resting. To "speak of the commandments" in daily rhythms was to root faith in real life.

Mishnah Insight:
"A home in which words of Torah are not heard will not endure."

— AVOT 1:11

This was not about religious performance, but consistent conversation. The Shema framed the day—spoken at morning and evening, over bread, during travel, through blessing.

Discipleship was domestic. And the home was holy ground.

Hebraic Terms Introduced This Week:

- **Bayit** – House; physical home and spiritual atmosphere
- **Devarim** – Words; often referring to God's words or commandments
- **Makor** – Source or spring; the home as the source of spiritual nurture

3. RECAP & REFLECTION (BOOK + DEVOTIONAL HIGHLIGHTS)

Book Recap – Hear, O Israel (Chapter 8):
This chapter emphasizes that faith isn't forged in formal spaces alone. It's in the car rides, bedtime routines, and kitchen conversations that the Shema truly takes root. The home becomes a sanctuary not by being perfect, but by being filled with the Word.

Devotional Tie-In – Listening in Love (Week 8):
This week's reflections explored how daily words shape discipleship. Day 3 shared the Mishnah insight on Torah in the home, and Day 4 told Micah's story—a child whose father blessed him every night with the Shema, and who passed that same blessing to his own child years later.

4. GROUP DISCUSSION QUESTIONS

Choose 4–6 questions that best fit your group:

1. *What stood out to you this week in the book or devotional?*
2. *How does the Shema reframe the idea of spiritual leadership in the home?*
3. *What kind of conversations happen most often in your household?*
4. *How do you currently invite God's Word into ordinary routines?*
5. *What memory shaped your view of faith in the home?*
6. *What could it look like to intentionally speak Scripture where you live?*

5. DUSTPRINT DISCIPLESHIP CHALLENGE

Invite your group to speak one intentional word of truth, Scripture, or blessing in their home every day this week.

Challenge Prompt (from Devotional):
"Let your home echo with heaven. Speak His Word in the place you live, and watch what begins to grow."

Examples:

- Bless your children or spouse aloud
- Share a Scripture at the table
- Begin or end the day with the Shema
- Speak life where frustration has filled the air

Encourage participants to reflect on what changed when God's words filled their space.

6. CLOSING PRAYER & GROUP BLESSING

Prayer Prompt:
God of every household, teach us to speak of You when we sit, rise, walk, and lie down. Let our homes reflect Your presence, not just through décor—but through devotion. May our rooms be filled with Your Word.
Amen.

Optional Group Blessing (spoken together):

"We speak the Word in our homes.
We shape the atmosphere with truth.
And our homes become places where the Shema lives."

SESSION 9: THE SHEMA AND THE MESSIAH

HOW JESUS FULFILLS AND REDEFINES THE SHEMA

Focus Verse

"The most important one," answered Jesus, "is this: 'Hear, O Israel: The Lord our God, the Lord is one.'"

— MARK 12:29

Theme: Jesus didn't replace the Shema—He fulfilled it. In Him, love becomes embodied, obedience becomes relational, and the covenant is made visible.

Leader Objective: By the end of this session, group members will be able to explain how Jesus rooted His teaching in the Shema, reflect on the connection between obedience and love in His ministry, and recognize where the Shema is being lived out through Christ in their own lives.

1. OPENING PRAYER & SHEMA

Prayer Prompt:
Jesus, You are the Living Word—the One who fulfilled the Shema not just in word, but in life. Teach us to love as You loved, obey as You obeyed, and reflect the unity of the Father in every step we take. Amen.

Optional Shema (Deuteronomy 6:4–5):
   "Hear, O Israel: The LORD our God, the LORD is one.
   Love the LORD your God with all your heart and with all your soul and with all your strength."

---

2. GROUNDING IN THE DUST (CULTURAL INSIGHT)

When Jesus was asked which commandment was greatest, He didn't create a new teaching—He quoted the Shema. This alone shows His rootedness in the Torah and the covenantal worldview of His people.

But Jesus added something: "Love your neighbor as yourself" (Leviticus 19:18). He brought together vertical loyalty and horizontal love—binding personal devotion and communal responsibility.

Mishnah Insight:
   "Accept upon yourself the yoke of the kingdom of heaven in the Shema."

— BERAKHOT 2:2

For early rabbis, reciting the Shema was an act of submission to God's kingship. For Jesus, it was the starting point for a life of relational love, radical forgiveness, and embodied obedience.

The Shema becomes fully alive when we see it in Jesus—and even more, when we live it through Him.

Hebraic Terms Introduced This Week:

- **Yoke (Ol)** – Rabbinic term for submission to a teacher's authority
- **Malkhut Shamayim** – Kingdom of Heaven
- **Halakhah** – "The way one walks"; the way a rabbi interpreted and lived Torah

3. RECAP & REFLECTION (BOOK + DEVOTIONAL HIGHLIGHTS)

Book Recap – Hear, O Israel (Chapter 9):
This chapter unpacks how Jesus didn't discard the Shema—He deepened it. Through His life, the Shema becomes incarnate: love in action, obedience from relationship, covenant in motion.

Devotional Tie-In – Listening in Love (Week 9):
Reflections this week focused on Jesus as the Living Shema. Day 3 featured a Mishnah insight about accepting the yoke of Heaven through the Shema, and Day 4 told the story of Malia—a woman who whispered her quiet "yes" to Jesus not with fanfare, but with surrendered trust.

4. GROUP DISCUSSION QUESTIONS

Choose 4–6 questions for your group to explore:

1. *What stood out to you from the reading or devotional this week?*
2. *Why do you think Jesus quoted the Shema as the "greatest commandment"?*
3. *How does seeing Jesus through the lens of the Shema deepen your understanding of His mission?*
4. *What does it mean to "accept the yoke" of Jesus in your daily life?*
5. *Where have you seen the Shema lived out in Christ's example—or in your own?*
6. *What part of Jesus' way of living the Shema is most challenging for you to follow?*

5. DUSTPRINT DISCIPLESHIP CHALLENGE

Encourage your group to choose one area of life where they can imitate Jesus this week—not through ritual, but through relational obedience.

Challenge Prompt (from Devotional):
"Live the Shema through Jesus' example. Choose one act of surrendered love—toward God or toward someone else—and follow through."

Examples:

- Forgive someone who's hard to forgive
- Serve quietly without seeking credit
- Spend time with someone on the margins
- Obey a prompting without delay

Ask your group to share reflections next week.

6. CLOSING PRAYER & GROUP BLESSING

Prayer Prompt:
Jesus, You are the fullness of the Shema. You listened, You obeyed, You loved. And now You call us to walk the same path. Help us follow You—not just in belief, but in how we love and live. Amen.

Optional Group Blessing (spoken together):
"We walk in the footsteps of the Messiah.
We love God with our whole being—and we love others as He has loved us."

SESSION 10: LOYALTY AMIDST IDOLATRY

FAITHFULNESS UNDER CULTURAL PRESSURE

FOCUS VERSE

"Do not follow other gods, the gods of the peoples around you."

— DEUTERONOMY 6:14

Theme: Loyalty to God is tested not just by trials, but by temptations to blend in, compromise, or drift. The Shema calls us to remain fully His—even when the culture bows elsewhere.

Leader Objective: By the end of this session, group members will be able to recognize modern expressions of idolatry, reflect on areas of divided loyalty, and commit to one act of bold obedience in a place where cultural pressure challenges faith.

1. OPENING PRAYER & SHEMA

Prayer Prompt:
God, we live in a world full of noise, pressure, and compromise. But we want to be fully Yours. Teach us to recognize the idols around us—and within us—and give us the courage to love You with undivided hearts.
Amen.

Optional Shema (Deuteronomy 6:4–5):
"Hear, O Israel: The LORD our God, the LORD is one.
Love the LORD your God with all your heart and with all your soul and with all your strength."

2. GROUNDING IN THE DUST (CULTURAL INSIGHT)

In the ancient Near East, idolatry was not just religious—it was cultural. To follow the gods of the surrounding nations was to align with their values, lifestyles, and power structures. The Shema stands in contrast: *the Lord is One*—and He alone is worthy of worship.

Talmud Insight:
"A man is not judged by the shout of battle, but by whom he serves when no one is watching."

— BERAKHOT 17A

Loyalty in Jewish thought was not proven by grand gestures but by everyday alignment. Idolatry today may not look like golden calves—but it lives in what we trust, fear, crave, and refuse to surrender.

Jesus reaffirmed this when He said, "No one can serve two masters" (Matthew 6:24). The Shema is a call to single-hearted allegiance.

Hebraic Terms Introduced This Week:

- **Avodah Zara** – Foreign worship; idolatry or misplaced devotion
- **Kavanah** – Intentionality or inner direction of the heart
- **Yirat Hashem** – Fear (reverence) of the Lord

3. RECAP & REFLECTION (BOOK + DEVOTIONAL HIGHLIGHTS)

Book Recap – Hear, O Israel (Chapter 10):
This chapter explores how Israel's greatest threat wasn't always persecution—but assimilation. We face the same danger today. Our loyalty is tested in quiet decisions: whose voice we follow, whose approval we seek, whose values we live by.

Devotional Tie-In – Listening in Love (Week 10):
This week's reflections named modern idols—control, applause, image, success. Day 3 featured the Talmudic insight about loyalty in the shadows, and Day 4 told the story of Darren—a man who slowly drifted into idolatry without realizing it until a single verse brought him back.

4. GROUP DISCUSSION QUESTIONS

Select 4–6 questions to guide the conversation:

1. *What impacted you most from this week's reading or devotional?*
2. *What are some modern "gods of the people around you" that tempt divided loyalty?*
3. *How can we tell when we've begun to blend our faith with cultural idols?*
4. *What is the difference between loud rebellion and quiet drift?*
5. *What role does reverence (yirat Hashem) play in keeping us aligned?*
6. *Where is God calling you to stand apart, even if it costs something?*

5. DUSTPRINT DISCIPLESHIP CHALLENGE

Invite your group to name and tear down one subtle idol this week—not with shame, but with courage.

Challenge Prompt (from Devotional):
"Choose one area of divided loyalty. Confront it. Confess it. Replace it with single-hearted love."

Examples:

- Delete a distraction that feeds comparison
- Say no to a commitment that competes with covenant
- Tithe from a place of fear
- Confess a cultural compromise in conversation or lifestyle

Encourage sharing next week on how it shifted their sense of alignment.

6. CLOSING PRAYER & GROUP BLESSING

Prayer Prompt:
Father, we repent of our divided hearts. We name the gods we've bowed to in secret—and we return to You. Let our loyalty be loud. Let our faith be full. And let our lives reflect that You alone are God.
Amen.

Optional Group Blessing (spoken together):
"We belong to the Lord alone.
We reject the idols of the age—and walk in covenant loyalty."

SESSION 11: COVENANT RENEWAL IN EXILE

REMEMBERING IDENTITY IN FOREIGN LANDS

Focus Verse

"But if from there you seek the Lord your God, you will find Him..."

— DEUTERONOMY 4:29

Theme: Exile does not erase covenant. God still calls, still listens, and still welcomes His people back—no matter how far they've gone.

Leader Objective: By the end of this session, group members will be able to name what "exile" looks like in their own journey, reflect on how God invites return, and take one step toward covenant renewal in their current context.

1. OPENING PRAYER & SHEMA

Prayer Prompt:
Lord, we've all known exile—places of distance, silence, or wandering. But You never stop calling. Let this session be a turning point. Draw us back to You, even from the farthest places.
Amen.

Optional Shema (Deuteronomy 6:4–5):
"Hear, O Israel: The LORD our God, the LORD is one.
Love the LORD your God with all your heart and with all your soul and with all your strength."

---

2. GROUNDING IN THE DUST (CULTURAL INSIGHT)

Exile (*galut*) was not only physical in the Hebrew worldview —it was also spiritual. It represented separation, disorientation, and the loss of home. Yet the covenant was never revoked.

In Jewish memory, God still hears the Shema even from Babylon. The people may be scattered, but God is not absent.

Midrash Insight:
"Even in exile, the voice of the Shema is not silenced. The Holy One hears from every land."

— DEVARIM RABBAH 2:25

This insight reminds us that identity isn't lost in foreign spaces—it's remembered there. Exile becomes the ground for renewal, if we seek Him "from there."

Hebraic Terms Introduced This Week:

- **Galut** – Exile; dislocation, scattering, or separation
- **Teshuvah** – Return or repentance; a turning back to covenant
- **Makom** – Place; also used as a name of God, "The Place" who holds us

3. RECAP & REFLECTION (BOOK + DEVOTIONAL HIGHLIGHTS)

Book Recap – Hear, O Israel (Chapter 11):
This chapter reminds us that exile is part of the biblical story —but not the end of it. The Shema is a call that continues even when we feel far from God. The invitation to return always remains open.

Devotional Tie-In – Listening in Love (Week 11):
The devotional led readers through themes of wandering, remembering, and coming home. Day 3 featured a Midrash about God hearing the Shema even in exile, and Day 4 told Kayla's story—how she recited the Shema from her car, too scared to walk into church, but finally ready to return.

4. GROUP DISCUSSION QUESTIONS

Choose 4–6 questions that resonate with your group:

1. *What part of this week's content hit home for you?*

2. *How would you describe "exile" in your life—past or present?*
3. *Why do you think God allows seasons of dislocation or silence?*
4. *What helps you remember covenant when you feel far from God?*
5. *What does teshuvah (return) look like in your current season?*
6. *What does it mean to believe the Shema still holds, even in exile?*

5. DUSTPRINT DISCIPLESHIP CHALLENGE

Challenge your group to take one step of return this week—a physical or spiritual action that represents coming back into covenant rhythm.

Challenge Prompt (from Devotional):
"Return from exile. From there—wherever 'there' is—begin again."

Examples:

- Reengage in a spiritual discipline that's faded
- Reenter a relationship, church, or space where you've distanced
- Confess where you've felt far—and let others help carry you back
- Whisper the Shema aloud each morning and night this week

Encourage group members to reflect on what "return" felt like by next session.

6. CLOSING PRAYER & GROUP BLESSING

Prayer Prompt:
Lord, You are the God who meets us "from there." From distant places, forgotten spaces, and broken rhythms—you still call us by name. We return to You now—not because we have it all together, but because You are faithful.
Amen.

Optional Group Blessing (spoken together):
"Even from exile, we return.
Our identity remains. Our covenant still stands. We are His people."

SESSION 12: LIVING THE SHEMA TODAY

EMBODYING COVENANTAL LOVE IN THE MODERN WORLD

Focus Verse

"Be careful to obey so that it may go well with you..."

— DEUTERONOMY 6:3

Theme: The Shema is not just an ancient confession—it's a present-day calling. It is meant to be lived in traffic, in tension, in parenting, in pain, in public, and in prayer.

Leader Objective: By the end of this session, group members will be able to reflect on how the Shema has shaped their journey, name one way they are living it more intentionally, and commit to a long-term rhythm of covenant faithfulness.

1. OPENING PRAYER & SHEMA

Prayer Prompt:
Lord, we've walked through these words—now help us live them.
Let the Shema not stay on the page, but take root in our hands, our
homes, and our hearts. May Your love be our rhythm.
Amen.

Optional Shema (Deuteronomy 6:4–5):
"Hear, O Israel: The LORD our God, the LORD is one.
Love the LORD your God with all your heart and with all
your soul and with all your strength."

---

2. GROUNDING IN THE DUST (CULTURAL INSIGHT)

The Shema was never intended to be a private creed. It was a communal rhythm—spoken aloud, remembered in motion, passed down from generation to generation. To "live the Shema" in today's world means to echo that rhythm in modern language, through modern obedience.

Talmud Insight:
"He who prolongs the word 'Echad' ('One') declares that
God is One in heaven and on earth, in every breath and in
every moment."

— BERAKHOT 13B

This insight teaches that God's oneness is not limited to spiritual settings. It applies to jobs, relationships, finances, social media, and silence.

Living the Shema today means choosing covenant wholeness where the world offers fragmentation.

Hebraic Terms Introduced This Week:

- **Echad** – One; the singular unity and kingship of God
- **Halakhah** – "The way one walks"; how belief becomes practice
- **Shalom** – Wholeness; the fruit of living in alignment with God's voice

3. RECAP & REFLECTION (BOOK + DEVOTIONAL HIGHLIGHTS)

Book Recap – Hear, O Israel (Chapter 12):
This final chapter invites readers to step beyond study into living. The Shema is a way of life: waking with purpose, choosing faithfulness, honoring God with decisions both big and small. The journey doesn't end here—it begins again, every morning.

Devotional Tie-In – Listening in Love (Week 12):
The devotional encouraged readers to reflect on the transformation of the last 12 weeks. Day 3 highlighted the Talmud's call to prolong "Echad"—to let God's oneness shape every moment. Day 4 told Sam's story—a quiet follower of Jesus whose daily habits became an echo of covenant love for generations.

4. GROUP DISCUSSION QUESTIONS

Choose 4–6 questions to celebrate the journey and set vision for what's next:

1. *What part of the Shema has impacted your life the most?*
2. *How has your view of "discipleship" shifted over the past 12 weeks?*
3. *In what area of your life has obedience become more natural?*
4. *Where are you still resisting covenant rhythm—and why?*
5. *What does "living the Shema" look like in your family, workplace, or city?*
6. *What rhythm or habit will you carry forward beyond this study?*

5. DUSTPRINT DISCIPLESHIP CHALLENGE

Encourage the group to identify one long-term practice they will commit to—something that helps them keep walking in the Shema every day.

Challenge Prompt (from Devotional):
"Don't just finish—continue. Choose one lasting rhythm of Shema-formed life."

Examples:

- Recite the Shema morning and night
- Read or memorize one verse weekly
- Begin Sabbath practices with family
- Volunteer regularly in a place of tension or need

- Create a rule of life based on heart, soul, and strength

Invite accountability or sharing of long-term commitments.

6. CLOSING PRAYER & GROUP BLESSING

Prayer Prompt:
God of covenant, thank You for meeting us in this journey. Thank You for Your voice, for Your Word, and for the path You've shown us. Help us to not merely hear—but live. To not merely remember—but embody. Let the Shema echo in every corner of our lives. Amen.

Optional Group Blessing (spoken together):
"We have heard. We will obey.
We live the Shema—in every step, every season, every breath.
He is One—and we are His."

EPILOGUE: STILL LISTENING

YOU'VE LED OTHERS THROUGH THE SHEMA—NOT JUST BY reading words, but by walking in rhythm. You've opened your Bible and your heart. You've wrestled with ancient truths and modern distractions. You've walked through stories, questions, and the dusty tension of obedience.

And now… you're not finished. You're formed.

This leader guide was never a script. It was a scaffold—a structure to support something far more eternal: covenant love.

You are a covenant guide. A modern talmid-maker. A disciple still learning, still leading, still listening.

As you continue to walk with others, remember this:

- You don't have to be perfect—you just have to be present.
- You don't need all the answers—you just need a posture of return.
- You don't lead alone—the Spirit is guiding even when you stumble.

The Shema is not a one-time prayer. It is a lifetime direction. A daily whisper. A tether in a world of noise.

So keep reciting it. Keep living it. Keep speaking it over homes, over children, over communities, over yourself.

Let your hands bear the dust of faithful steps. Let your home carry the sound of Scripture. Let your strength become offering. Let your soul remain open. Let your heart stay aligned.

And above all—let your life continue to say:

"Hear, O Israel: The Lord is our God. The Lord is One.
And we love Him—with everything we are."

You're still listening.
And so is He.

- **Leading the Exodus People:** *A Leader's Companion to The Exodus Still Echoes*

MARTIAL ARTS WORKS

Warrior Spirit: *Incorporating Biblical Teachings into Your Martial Arts Journey*

Covenant Warrior Adaptations

Including forthcoming titles such as expanded, covenant-rooted adaptations of classical works like **The Art of War**, **The Book of Five Rings**, *and* **The Bubishi**, *reimagined for the modern Christian martial artist.*